21st Century
Basic Skills
Library

HOW'S THE WEATHER IN SPRING?

by Jenna Lee Gleisner

Cherry Lake Publishing • Ann Arbor, Michigan

1

Published in the United States of America
by Cherry Lake Publishing
Ann Arbor, Michigan
www.cherrylakepublishing.com

Consultant: Marla Conn, ReadAbility, Inc.

Photo Credits: iStockphoto, Cover, Title, 12; Shutterstock Images, 4, 6;
Samuel Borges Photography/Shutterstock Images, 8, 14, 16, 18, 20;
Alexander Shadrin/Shutterstock Images, 10

Library of Congress Cataloging-in-Publication Data
Gleisner, Jenna Lee.
  How's the weather in spring? / by Jenna Lee Gleisner.
     pages cm. -- (Let's look at spring)
  Audience: 5-7.
  Audience: K to grade 3.
  Includes index.
  ISBN 978-1-62431-654-8 (hardcover) -- ISBN 978-1-62431-681-4 (pbk.) --
ISBN 978-1-62431-708-8 (pdf) -- ISBN 978-1-62431-735-4 (hosted ebook)
  1. Spring--Juvenile literature. 2. Weather--Juvenile literature. I. Title.

QB637.5.G54 2014
551.6--dc23

                                        2013029052

Cherry Lake Publishing would like to acknowledge
the work of The Partnership for 21st Century Skills.
Please visit www.p21.org for more information.

Printed in the United States of America
Corporate Graphics Inc.
January 2014

TABLE OF CONTENTS

Spring Changes

Spring comes after winter.
It brings many changes.

Warm

The **temperature** rises. Warm weather helps plants and leaves grow.

Tyson feels the warmer weather. He plays outside at the park.

10

Rain

Clouds hold water. When there is too much water, it falls. We call these drops of water rain.

What Do You See?

What color is Kay's raincoat?

12

Lots of rain falls in spring. Kay wears a raincoat to stay dry.

Plants need rain. It keeps **soil** wet. Now plants can grow big!

Sunlight

The sun rises earlier in spring. It goes down later. There is more sunlight.

What Do You See?

How many buds do you see?

Sun and rain help plants grow. New **buds** grow on tree branches.

What Do You See?

What kind of flower do you see?

20

Spring days get warmer.
Summer is almost here!

Find Out More

BOOK

Herrington, Lisa M. *How Do You Know It's Spring?* New York: Children's Press, 2014.

WEB SITE

PBS Kids

www.pbskids.org/sid/weatherwheel.html

Spin the weather wheel and help Gerald dress for the different seasons.

Glossary

buds (BUHDZ) small bumps on a plant that grow into leaves or flowers

soil (SOIL) the top layer of earth where plants grow

temperature (TEM-pur-uh-chur) how hot or cold something is

Home and School Connection

Use this list of words from the book to help your child become a better reader. Word games and writing activities can help beginning readers reinforce literacy skills.

big	grow	shorts	warm
branches	leaves	soil	water
brings	outside	spring	weather
buds	park	summer	wet
changes	plants	sun	winter
clouds	plays	sunlight	
drops	rain	temperature	
dry	raincoat	tree	

What Do You See?

What Do You See? is a feature paired with select photos in this book. It encourages young readers to interact with visual images in order to build the ability to integrate content in various media formats.

You can help your child further evaluate photos in this book with additional activities. Look at the images in the book without the What Do You See? feature. Ask your child to point out one detail in each image, such as a color, time of day, animal, or setting.

Index

About the Author

Jenna Lee Gleisner is an editor and author who lives in Minnesota. She loves when spring comes to Minnesota! It melts away the snow and brings warm weather so she can take her dog for long walks around the lake.